RACECARS

By Russ Flint

IDEALS CHILDREN'S BOOKS

Copyright © 1989 by Ideals Publishing Corporation

All rights reserved.

Printed and bound in the United States of America.

Published by Ideals Publishing Corporation

Nashville, Tennessee

ISBN 0-8249-8307-6

THE INDY CAR

Car number seven is out of fuel and needs new tires. The pit crew dressed in white will have to work fast to get the car back into the race.

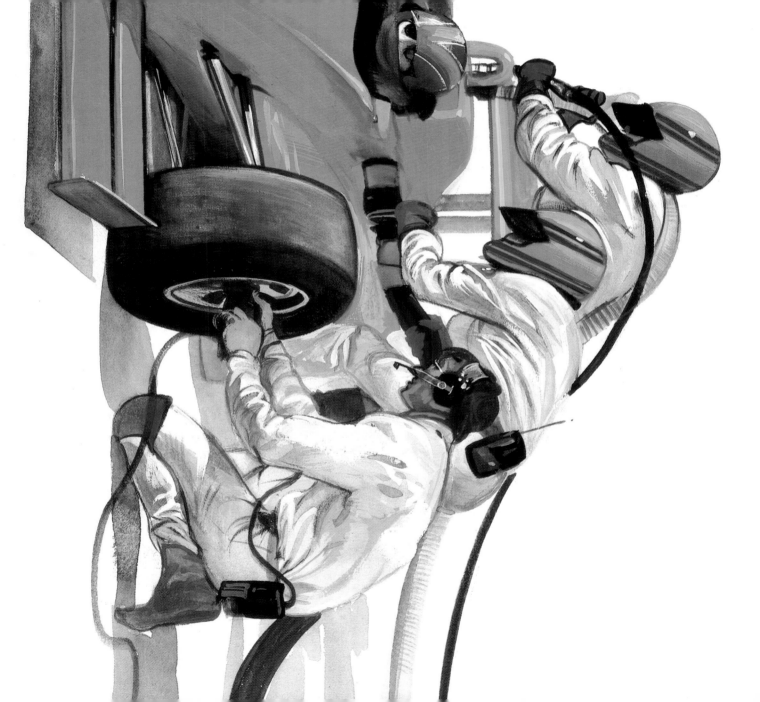

THE FORMULA ONE CAR

Like the Indy car, the formula one car races on a smooth, paved track. This car is low to the ground and is very fast!

THE GTP CAR

Racecars have the names of their sponsors lettered on them. Sponsors pay to help keep the cars racing.

THE DRAGSTER

The dragster races in a straight line down a long, paved strip.

The nose of a dragster is long and pointed to cut through the air, and the weight of the engine and driver is centered over the rear wheels. The wind rushes over and around the wing on the back of the car and pushes it closer to the ground, making for better traction.

The rear tires spin so fast that they get very hot and burn in clouds of thick, black smoke.

PRO STOCK

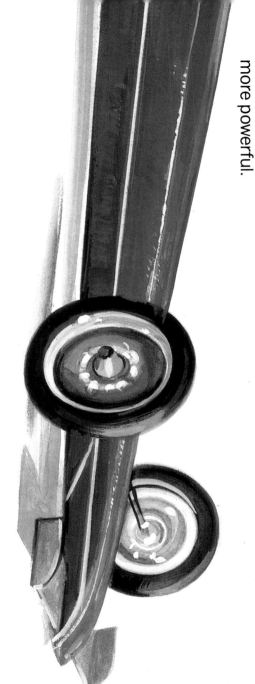

The air scoop on the hood of this racer allows more air to flow into the engine, causing better combustion which makes the engine more powerful.

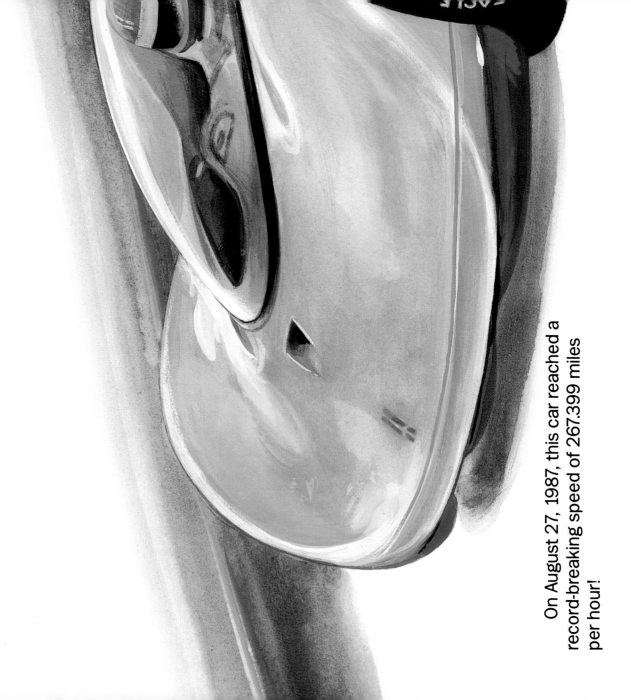

RECORD BREAKER

On August 27, 1987, this car reached a record-breaking speed of 267.399 miles per hour!

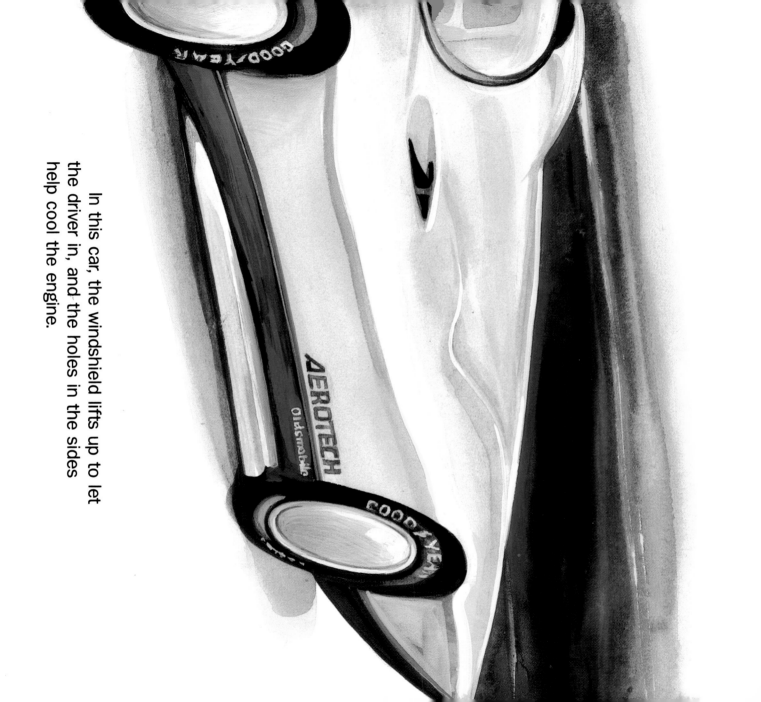

In this car, the windshield lifts up to let the driver in, and the holes in the sides help cool the engine.

THE GTO CAR

Even the family car can be turned into a racecar. This car races on paved tracks from one to four miles long. The GTO car can reach speeds of over 200 miles per hour.

THE STOCK CAR

Most ordinary cars are too light to race very fast. A "nose piece" has been added to the front bumper of this car to direct the air over the car. The pressure from this air helps hold the car on the ground when it's racing at top speed.

THE SPRINT CAR

Sprint cars race on both paved and dirt tracks. Many sprint cars have large aluminum wings on top of the cars. Some even have wings in front. No two sprint cars look very much alike.

THE MIDGET

These cars may be small, but watch out! They are almost as fast as the Indy Cars.

DESERT RACERS

THE JEEP

Jeeps aren't very fast, but they are strong and dependable. The yellow discs on the front are protective covers for the lights.

THE CLASS TWO UNLIMITED

This car looks like a bug on the desert sand. It is built so that the frame is high enough to clear rough terrain. When it hits a bump, it jumps high into the air and then drops back to earth. It can cross almost any terrain at high speed.

RACING TRUCKS

Both big and little trucks race just like cars do. These two trucks carry spare tires in the back.

Acknowledgments

Our thanks to the following for permission to artistically reproduce the cars contained in this book: Cover, Deke Houlgate; Indy Car, Art Flores; Formula One Car, USF&G; Dragster, Ron Lewis, Bill Barney; Dragster, Ford Motor Company; GTO, Ford Motor Company; Record Breaker, Oldsmobile Corporation; Sprint Racer, Art Flores; Midget Racer, John Mahoney; Desert Racer, Lane Evans; 4-Wheel Racer, Pete Biro; Racing Trucks, Ford Motor Company.